Stay Healthy! Learn To Look After Your Body

By Amani Uduman

Illustrated by Begum Manav

Library For All Ltd.

Library For All is an Australian not for profit organisation with a mission to make knowledge accessible to all via an innovative digital library solution. Visit us at libraryforall.org

Stay Healthy! Learn To Look After Your Body

First published 2022

Published by Library For All Ltd
Email: info@libraryforall.org
URL: libraryforall.org

This work is licensed under the Creative Commons Attribution-NonCommercial-NoDerivatives 4.0 International License. To view a copy of this license, visit http://creativecommons.org/licenses/by-nc-nd/4.0/.

This book was made possible by the generous support of the June Canavan Foundation.

Original illustrations by Begum Manav plus stock photos

Stay Healthy! Learn To Look After Your Body
Uduman, Amani
ISBN: 978-1-922795-94-6
SKU04093

Stay Healthy! Learn To Look After Your Body

Staying healthy

Do you know why it's important to stay healthy? When we feel healthier, we feel happier. We find it easier to learn and play because our body has more energy.

And if you do get sick, a healthy body will help you to get better sooner. So, let's talk about how to stay healthy!

Healthy food

Eating a variety of food, such as fresh fruit and vegetables, lean meat, seafood, and poultry will help you gain all the nutrients for your body to be strong.

There are also a variety of meat-free options such as beans, soy, lentils, and other legumes for people that are vegetarian or trying to reduce meat in their diet.

TRY TO EAT EVERY COLOUR OF THE RAINBOW.

WHICH HEALTHY FOOD SHOULD TAM CHOOSE?

Water matters

Water is important for a healthy diet.

It may be difficult to drink enough water throughout the day but making it a habit can help.

A good idea is to drink when you're thirsty and after exercising. This helps restore the balance of water in your body.

> THE AMOUNT OF WATER IN A HUMAN BODY RANGES FROM 45-75 PER CENT.

How much should I drink?

It is recommended that the daily intake of water for children is:

1
- 5 to 8 years old: 5 glasses (1 litre)

2
- 9 to 12 years old: 7 glasses (1.5 litres)

3
- 13 years old and over: 8 to 10 glasses (2 litres)

Safe drinking water

When people don't have safe tap or bottled water, they boil the water and let it cool down, before drinking it. This kills off any bacteria and parasites that could make people ill. It's best to ask an adult to help you when handling boiled water.

WATER BOILS WHEN IT REACHES 100° CELSIUS

Exercise

WHICH EXERCISE WOULD YOU LIKE TO DO?

DID YOU KNOW?

1

Exercise has many benefits such as keeping you fit and helping to build a stronger body.

2

Exercise also helps reduce body fat and helps you get a better night's sleep.

3

Exercise can be as simple as going for a walk or playing games outside in the yard.

4

Get your body moving and have fun at the same time! It's great for your body and your mind.

Germs

A healthy person can fight off germs from the world around them.

Germs are tiny living organisms that can cause disease in our bodies.

People that lack nutrients in their body have weaker immune systems and can fall ill more easily.

FISH AND POTATOES ARE EXAMPLES OF NUTRIENT-PACKED FOODS.

Nutrients provide us with energy.

Nutrients help us to grow.

Nutrients are compounds in food that help our bodies work properly.

Nutrients help our body to repair itself from cuts or injuries.

MACRONUTRIENTS

Carbohydrates　　　　Proteins　　　　Fats

Nutrients include

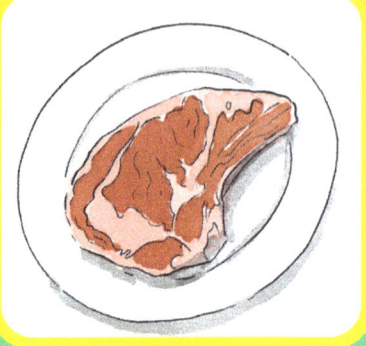

Proteins found in meat, seafood, dairy, legumes, and eggs.

Carbohydrates found in rice, pasta, potatoes, milk, and fruit.

Lipids (known as fats) found in oils, butter, margarine, seeds, nuts, meat, and seafood.

Nutrients include

Vitamins found in a variety of food including fruits, vegetables, grains, cereals, full-fat diary, and egg yolks.

Minerals including calcium, sodium, and iron to name a few, are found in a variety of foods.

Water is found in many fruits and vegetables and as a drink.

Hygiene

With the spread of diseases in our communities, it is important to keep your body as healthy as it can be. You can also look after your family and friends and stop the spread of germs by doing a few simple things.

RUB YOUR HANDS TOGETHER, AND SQUISH THE SOAP BETWEEN YOUR FINGERS.

Start by washing your hands often using soap and water. Wash them before eating and after going to the toilet. Wash them when doing things around the house and when returning home from school.

GERMS CAN SURVIVE UP TO THREE HOURS ON YOUR HANDS!

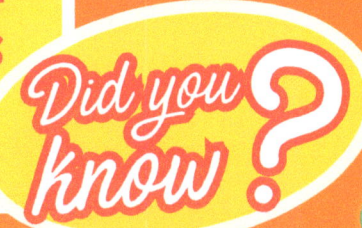

What else can you do?

Cover your nose and mouth with a tissue when you need to cough, spit or sneeze. Used tissues should be thrown in the bin. It's always best practice to wash your hands afterwards. This will help your family and friends from falling sick.

NO TISSUE, NO PROBLEM.

If you don't have a tissue, you could cough or sneeze into your elbow and not onto your hands. If you need to spit, you should go to a washroom if possible.

A SNEEZE CAN LEAVE YOUR BODY AT UP TO 160 KM/H!

Keep your distance

1 Try not to visit friends and family that are unwell.

2 Wear a face mask when in a crowded place or when your community leaders tell you to do so.

3 A cloth face mask will need to be washed often, while it is recommended that a surgical or paper face mask should be used only once.

4 Not sharing drink containers with your family and friends such as bottled or canned drinks, cups and even straws.

5 Keeping a 1.5 metre distance from other people when in a crowded place and when out of the house. This is important even if people don't show any signs or symptoms of being sick as they may still be infected or be a possible carrier.

6 Choosing open aired places over closed spaces. When indoors, open a window.

7 Staying home if you're feeling unwell.

What if you get sick?

If you have difficulty breathing or you start feeling very unwell, your family and friends can help you get medical advice from your doctor.

TRUST YOUR DOCTOR, NOT SOCIAL MEDIA, FOR HEALTH ADVICE!

CAN YOU FIND ALL THE THINGS THAT PEOPLE ARE DOING CORRECTLY?

Stay safe, stay healthy and look after your family and friends!

Photo Credits

Page	Details
Cover, Title page & p. 4	Pixabay/Pfüderi/ID: 2364221
p. 6	Pixabay/JackSellaire/ID: 3588739
p. 8	Shutterstock.com/ID: 156916754
p. 12	Pixabay/ReinhardThainer/ID: 5037330
p. 13	Shutterstock.com/Andrii Bezvershenko/ID: 1573379986
p. 16	Shutterstock.com/wavebreakmedia/ID: 1983750128
p. 17	Prostock-studio/ID: 1105252997
p. 18	Shutterstock.com/Bernardo Emanuelle/ID: 1733059286
p. 19	Shuttertock.com/Drazen Zigic/ID: 1798168345
p. 22	Pixabay/Pixelkult/ID: 998990
p. 24	Shutterstock/The Road Provides/ID: 1515808061

You can use these questions to talk about this book with your family, friends and teachers.

What did you learn from this book?

Describe this book in one word. Funny? Scary? Colourful? Interesting?

How did this book make you feel when you finished reading it?

What was your favourite part of this book?

download our reader app
getlibraryforall.org

About the author

Amani Uduman migrated to Australia from Sri Lanka, with her family, when she was five years old. She studied at Deakin University, Melbourne, and obtained a degree in teaching. Being a busy mum of three children, she loves writing stories in her spare time. She also enjoys reading children's stories that are quirky, imaginative, and fun.

Did you enjoy this book?

We have hundreds more expertly curated original stories to choose from.

We work in partnership with authors, educators, cultural advisors, governments and NGOs to bring the joy of reading to children everywhere.

Did you know?

We create global impact in these fields by embracing the United Nations Sustainable Development Goals.

libraryforall.org

www.ingramcontent.com/pod-product-compliance
Lightning Source LLC
Chambersburg PA
CBHW040315050426
42452CB00018B/2859